The Old

Black Cat

A Witch's Pocket Guide
to Superstitious Magic

Roger J. Horne

Also by Roger J. Horne:

A Gathering of Witches: Sorcerous Folktales & Curious Accounts

The Charmer's Root: Witching Ways with Common Flora

The Witches' Devil: Myth and Lore for Modern Cunning

A Broom at Midnight: 13 Gates of Witchcraft by Spirit Flight

The Witch's Art of Incantation: Spoken Charms, Spells, & Curses in Folk Witchcraft

Cartomancy in Folk Witchcraft: Playing Cards and Marseille Tarot in Divination, Magic, & Lore

Folk Witchcraft: A Guide to Lore, Land, & the Familiar Spirit for the Solitary Practitioner

Contents

Introduction

For those who practice the good, old arts of folk magic, our first education comes early. *Toss a coin into a fountain*, many of us are told, *and make a wish*. The simplicity of this practice, passed down from parents and grandparents across the New World and British Isles, belies the depth and complexity of its origins. Coin magic is ancient, and comes in many iterations around the world, often to do with pocket-charms intended to attract more coin one's way. The common practice of making a wish as one throws a coin into a fountain is at least as old as ancient Rome, where such pagan practices were commonplace. Similar traditions of tossing coins into holy wells or ponds are likely prehistoric in origin, and are widespread across the British Isles. These rites were originally intended as an offering to a local spirit, or *genius locus*, dwelling in a body of water, most likely in exchange for its blessing and its favor. This ancient ritual, though simple, has survived via a simple, everyday practice, evolving over centuries, across generations, delivered to us so gently, so subtly, that it became an everyday act of magic hidden in plain sight.

And yet, modern magical practice often revolves around anything but the cultural traditions passed down this way. Instead, we are told that we must purchase special ceremonial robes and invest in endless arrays of expensive magical tools, that the magic we seek must be found in costly seminars led by self-appointed gurus, that magic is not a part of who we are already, but must be sought outside of ourselves, often at great expense. And still, something in us is hungry for more, for something that feels real, that feels like home. Something that glimmers with the magic we remember from childhood, something simple and true, something unpretentious and full of feeling, some magic that feels as warm and familiar as the voice of a loving grandmother wrapping her arms around us.

These magics are available to us at all times. In fact, they are already a part of us. Your folk magic, of course, will be different from mine. My ancestors are from Western Scotland and the Appalachian Mountains of the New World, and the histories of these peoples and these places are woven into the everyday magics I keep. But even within one's cultural roots, individual families develop their own interpretation of shared traditions, and what's more, individual practitioners who keep alive the old folk ways inevitably arrive at their own personal interpretations of charms. All of this variation is natural, and more importantly, it is *good*, because it means that the tradition is not only preserved, but is actually *alive and well*, adapting and shifting and thriving in the living descendants of those old charmers from an age before.

The importance of superstitious observance to pagan practice cannot be overstated. The word *superstition* comes from Latin, roughly translated as a belief that has "stood over" or stayed in its place long after its cultural context of belief has vanished or been replaced by a new ideology. In other words, superstitions have always been understood, since ancient times, as relics of older spiritual practices. Within these relics, there still lies a spark of magic. Just as the popular image of the witch is composed of actual elements of historical magical practice—largely derived from cunning folk, healers, and the collective memory of prehistoric shamanic practices—so, too, are superstitions derived from the actual magical practices of generations past. In rekindling the magical charms at the heart of surviving superstitions, we honor the dead who have carried the spark forward, and we reach into the past in order to connect with the magics of our own ancestors and our own cultures.

For a small number of folk practitioners, our practice goes a step further and falls under what is called *folk witchery*. For us, the traditions we keep are at the heart of the figure of the folkloric witch—practices related to spirit communication, pact-making, seasonal observances, spirit flight, dream journeying, and sorceries both light and dark. Every folk witch practices some variety of folk magic, but not every folk magician is a folk *witch*. I will not step into the nasty business of defining here who is a witch and who is not, for this question is contextual and differs widely among cultures. A witch with roots in cunning craft may engage in workings that a fairy doctoring witch does not, just as the craft of a Mexican bruja may not look quite like the practice of an Italian strega. Many of us have cultural roots that are mingled, and so we may draw, respectfully and lovingly, from multiple cultural traditions that have shaped us. Suffice it to say that the folklore and superstitions of every culture define, in some way, what it is that *witches* do, and it is in these specific differences that the practice of folk witchery may be found within one's own cultural roots.

Some of these trappings of the old folk witchery have become readily recognizable. There is a reason, for example, that witches are popularly associated with brooms, black cats, and the ancient festival that survives to this day as All Hallows' Eve. The superstitions of brooms and black cats reveal a very clear link to old magical practices of warding, protection, and divination, many of which are noted in the second half of this very volume. And All Hallows' Eve, of all the magical days of the year, features perhaps most heavily in superstitions to do with the arts of augury and spirit contact. The modern image of the witch is associated with these things because these magical practices survived among real people for a very long time.

But the work of folk witchery is more than the mere task of acquiring charms and magical knowledge. If stepping onto the path of witchcraft is an act of resistance against religious and moral authority— which it *always* is—then stepping into folk witchery is an act of resistance against other modern forms of authority. We are defining what is valuable in our craft not by how expensive, trendy, or fashionable something is, but by nearness and dearness to the *folk*, to our people, our ancestors, our cultures, and our lands. We are consecrating as sacred the words and actions of our people, people who were not rich or famous, not billionaires or CEOs or celebrities. Our folk aren't precious to us because of what they achieved or what they earned; they are precious because they are *ours*, because we belong to them, and they to us.

Religious leaders tell us to spend our lives spreading their gospels, expanding their power and influence in order to earn the salvation they promise. Corporate leaders tell us to spend our lives and our meager wages in their machinery, that we might earn our place among the rich. In a rising, disturbing trend, social influencers tell us to spend our lives embodying their aesthetic in order to earn more social capital, to make ourselves more magnetic and desirable to others. Folk craft is an antidote to these poisons. It turns all of these value systems on their heads. Folk witchery tells us to value *people*, to see the inherent value that already exists in the cultural traditions that shape us. There is nothing external to earn or attain, only the opportunity to settle deeper into ourselves, to connect with our inherent magics and the treasures thereof, passed down by loving ancestors. This is the real work hidden behind the practical task of rekindling charms from the old lore: we are reconsecrating the old stories and voices of everyday people, making them sacred once again.

For practical reasons, this book focuses on the superstitious magical practices of people in the British Isles and the New World. This focus is intended to be respectful, not exclusionary. I believe it would be irresponsible of me to pretend to grasp the intricacies of other cultures well enough to convey them properly, and so I leave that work in the capable hands of others. But I also believe that the logical conclusion of folk craft is not nationalism or xenophobia, but empathy; by connecting with our own cultural roots, by lifting up the magics and memories of our own folk, we acknowledge, implicitly, the dignity and reverence that *all* folk traditions deserve. Once we cease imagining that all folk magics belong to us, once we connect again with our own roots, we can begin to appreciate the distinct flavor and personality of traditions that are not our own, to respect them as sister traditions, carried on by their own practitioners in their own cultural milieu, no less precious than our own.

This work is intended as a sampling, a basic starting point, with a breadth limited by its small size, so that it may be carried anywhere—perhaps in a bag or purse where it can be "at the ready," or perhaps in a table drawer where one keeps a small candle and a bag of salt, just in case. A "pocket guide" may not be comprehensive, but it can be eminently useful. Despite this book's deceptively small stature, I believe that inquisitive, intelligent practitioners will note its many avenues of use, both as an index of magical superstitions and a basic primer on developing one's own innovative charm work that is grounded in historical magic.

How to Use This Book

This little book is divided roughly into two parts. The first part contains instructions for drawing on superstitious practices in order to rekindle their flame as magical rituals for various effects. It is designed to help you build your own unique, personal practice of superstitious folk witchery. The second, lengthier part is an index of sorts, containing over 400 superstitions of the British Isles and the New World, organized by topic, and arranged by region.

I recommend beginning here, with the rudimentary instructions for developing one's own practice of folk charming, perhaps making side notes in the margins for future reference or stuffing slips of paper between its pages with scribbled tips and shortcut rituals of one's own design, based on the guidance provided. Follow the instructions for developing basic rituals for routine use, and write your own on a slip of paper tucked inside.

Next, flag key superstitions in the second half, noting items that are familiar to you, superstitions that you may have heard growing up, relics that may be rich with potential for the development of charms later. As you develop individual charms towards various ends, write them down, and stuff those slips of paper into the appropriate sections, so that you can flip to them easily in times of need.

Once you have developed your own ritual structure and a healthy smattering of practical charms from familiar superstitions, look through the bibliography at the end of this book to find additional collections of superstitions that you may wish to visit. Pore through these at your leisure (many are available online for free via libraries and archives), noting additional items that are suggestive of practical spells you might wish to use. Let your repertoire grow, and experiment with your magic freely, developing your own interpretations of these age-old charms.

This book is not an office ledger or a pristine family bible. Please, by all means, make a mess of the thing. Wear its edges until they go soft. Stuff its pages with scraps of paper until the cover bulges. Tie it with a ribbon, or stretch a rubber band over it to hold it together once it swells and loosens. Make it your own, and allow it to become warped and faded with use. If, down the line, you find that you have developed quite a collection of spells, you may wish to purchase a simple blank journal and transcribe them into your own grimoire, as practitioners of the magical arts have done for hundreds of years. But if this feels too fussy for you, fret not. The tradition of building upon existing grimoires by scribbling in them and tucking in new pages has existed for just as long. In fact, many of the historical grimoires of magic that have survived to this day are made up of just this sort of stuff: the work of one practitioner building on another, making notes and adding items to an existing magical tome.

€ngaging the Magical Senses

efore we can engage in any form of magic, superstitiously derived or not, we must be able to *feel* spiritual forces around us. Without our magical senses, we are doomed to failure in our craft, like a painter wearing a blindfold. If you have already developed your magical senses, or if you were fortunate enough to be born with them, feel free to skip this exercise. If, however, you are a person who has never felt spiritual power in your life and cannot bring yourself to believe that there is magic in you already, then the following exercise is meant for you.

To begin, go to a private room in your home where you will not be disturbed for at least half an hour. Ensure that there will be no noises or interruptions. Light a single candle, and block out all other light so that the candle is the only source of illumination in the room. Remove any rings or jewelry on your hands and wrists, and sit comfortably before the candle, either at a table or desk or on the floor, if that is comfortable for your body.

Take several deep breaths, and relax. For the next half hour, the only thing that matters is you. Let everything outside of the candle's light disappear into the darkness. It will all still be there when you return to it, so for now, let it go, and focus only on your body, the candle, and the darkness around you.

Now, focus on the rhythm of your breath. Let it become deep and slow. Don't force it; breathe comfortably and naturally. Bring your two hands together as if in prayer, and begin sliding your palms against one another, back and forth, as if you were rubbing oil between them. Let the gliding of your hands become synchronized with your slow breaths.

Allow your mind to believe that there is actually a substance between your hands, an invisible layer outside of the skin itself. It is very thin, invisible to the naked eye, but it is there. As you rub your hands together, falling deeper into the rhythm of your breath, you may feel something like static between your hands, a slight tingle and warmth.

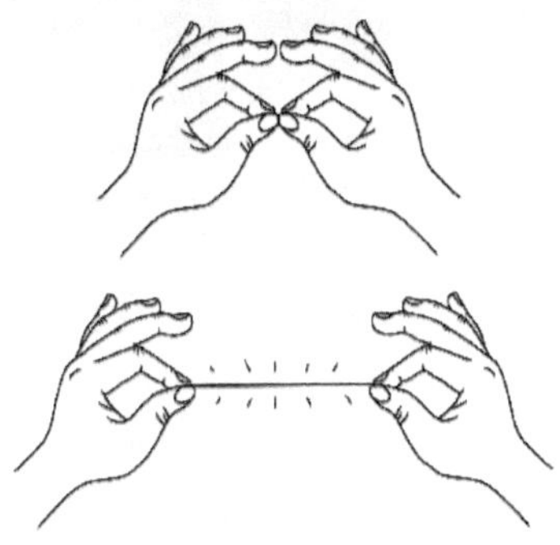

With your dominant hand, pinch the tips of your index finger and thumb together, as if you are holding a very fine thread. Do the same with the other hand. Bring your two hands together so that these four fingertips are now touching.

Now, pull your hands apart again very, very, *very* slowly, and continue pinching as if you are stretching out a taut length of thread. It is a very fine thread, so fine that you cannot see it with the naked eye in this dark room. Continue pulling your hands apart (*very* slowly) until they are about shoulder-width apart. Now hold, and focus your sight (not your *eyes*, but your *sight*) on the space between. Can you perceive the thread? It is difficult to describe how it looks exactly, but you will know it instinctively. It may look like a *there* that is not *there*. You may perceive it as a thread-thin warp in the space before you, like an absence of a thing rather than a thing itself. It may look slightly blue, or off-blue, like the impressions you see on the backs of your eyelids after looking at a bright light.

Even if you cannot "see" the thread yet, you will most likely be able to *feel* it. Still holding your hands in the same position, try moving one hand away (again, *very* slowly). Notice how even without meaning to, the other hand moves very slightly in the same direction, as if it is being pulled along by the thread. It will probably be a very slight movement, just a tiny budge really, but it is enough to be noticeable.

There is, of course, no thread at all. Or rather, the thread exists only for you. Let me explain. This exercise isn't about manipulating energy or hidden electromagnetic fields. It's about *belief* and *interdependence.* When you rubbed your hands together and focused on drawing out the thread, you established a connection between your hands that could be felt and perceived because our perception of the world is a malleable thing. On such a small level, some might call this a "trick of the mind," but the same rules apply to quite large things, things everyone sees and experiences, things that are very real by any definition. The thread you felt isn't a "trick" anymore than love is a trick. Just like love, magic is actually a foundational aspect of the human experience.

Most of our popular beliefs about magic come from fantasy and science fiction. We are told that magic is supernatural, that it exists outside of nature and our physical bodies. This isn't the case. Magic is not supernatural, but *preternatural*, which is to say, it exists at the very limits of what we know about nature and about ourselves—still inside of what is possible by the laws of nature, but just at the limit of what we understand. And it operates based on rules that are defined collectively, in a reality constructed by many threads of magic, a kind of tapestry that we are always weaving together, a fabric that we call *life*.

The threads of magic are always around us. There are threads we inherit that define how we understand and operate in the world from a young age. There are threads made and upheld by institutions, governing bodies, religions, and organizations. These threads are strong. There are threads of tradition, consisting of superstitions, values, and collectively-held beliefs. These are even stronger. There are threads of our own making, ideas we have about who we are and what we need. There are threads made by others around us, defining themselves for themselves. And there are threads between us, connecting us, one to another.

When you pull one end of a thread, whatever lies on the other end *moves*. The stronger the thread, the more pronounced the movement will be. This is the essence of magic, and it is neither supernatural nor fictive in any sense. It is an embodied, plain reality, a part of the world we live in. It's just that we often don't perceive magic when it is at work around us, the same way we aren't always consciously aware of the ground under our feet. I have used the thread as a metaphor, but this same principle is at the heart of the concept of magical correspondence and the old doctrine of signatures, the idea that *like affects like*, that connected things bear some effect upon one another that can be felt and utilized.

What of spirits, then? What of the dead, the ancestors, the gods? What of the spirits of the grimoires, called "angels" or "demons" depending on the perspective of the practitioner? What of the spirits of places, of hills and streams? What of the spirits of animals and plants? Are they constructed things, spun from the threads of magic that we are always weaving together, or have they always existed? In the ancient world, both were true. The patron deity of a community, for example, was considered very real, but if the city was conquered and the effigy of that god was desecrated by the enemy, the people wept for its spirit. Perhaps the relationship between humans and spirits is more complex than the simplistic dichotomy of creature or creator, master or servant, constructed or eternal. Witches frequently rely on the aid of spirits who are considered "kin," sharing something of our nature, our values, our personality, or our heritage. But perhaps the spirits also need us. Perhaps that relationship, in its healthiest form, is not one of subservience on either end, but of reciprocity, kinship, or even love.

Psychologists, more than any other academics, do seem to understand something of magic and spiritual entities. They may use modern academic terms to explain magical events and beliefs, but much of their discipline is about the study of the same forces. Let's admit, though, that magic is older than psychology. It has always been a part of the human experience. Often, magical practitioners and psychologists explore the same concepts in different language, but we must remember that magic is not merely cause and effect; it is also *spiritual and cultural tradition*. It is not a science, but an art. Not an experiment, but a creative belonging, a continuation of the workings of our own magical ancestors. In short, magic is both a natural phenomenon of the world, with all the practical uses we might imagine, *and* a folk art, a tradition survived in real people that can help us to connect or reconnect with who we are and where we come from. And the threads of tradition are strong, stronger than any thread we may make for ourselves alone, for many hands went into their making, over many generations.

Opening Rituals

Usually, acts of magic begin with some form of opening ritual. The function of this ritual, which can be quite simple, is to signal to the spiritual forces around us that the words and acts that follow are more than mundane. In opening rituals, we alert the spirits we consider kin, be they ancestors, guides, gods, or simply local land spirits, that we are beginning a series of actions that are of *interest to them*. Our goal is to get the spirits around us to pay attention. On a more immediate level, we are training our mind to shift back and forth between magical and mundane consciousness on command, so that we are not catapulted unexpectedly into encounters with the spirit world, but rather, are able to control when and where we awaken that part of ourselves. Remember that the threads of tradition are strong, and this is the heart of folk magic, so let's examine some elements of this tradition in order to ground our practice in those old superstitious threads of generations past.

In Scottish tradition, there exist a great many spoken charms called Paternosters, which are employed to various effects. One variant of what is called the Black Paternoster is probably already known to you, or at least the following portion of it:

> *Four corners round my bed.*
> *Four angels round my head.*
> *One to watch, and one to pray,*
> *And two to bear my soul away.*

Though grim stuff, the concept behind this spoken charm is quite plain: we are surrounded at each cardinal direction by spirits who will guard us, and if harm befalls us, carry our soul safely to the afterlife. This focus on spiritual allies conjured from four directions is a hallmark of the ritual form we're after.

We see this directional focus more formally in works in the grimoiric tradition, such as the *Heptameron* of Peter de Abano, a manual of practical magic and spirit conjuration from the 17th century:

> *...Let [the magician] enter the circle, and call the angels from the four corners of the world, which do govern the seven planets and the seven days of the week, colours and metals...Then let [the magician] call the angels from the four parts of the world that rule the air the same day wherein he doth the work or experiment...*

It is clear in the remainder of the grimoire that these so-called "angels" are not the sweet cherubs of modern Christianity, but frightening figures often described with weapons and terrifying features. Many of the "angels" of the Heptameron are actually fallen spirits, which is to say demons. (And these "demons" themselves, as a side note, are often derived from old pagan deities, survived in diminished and villainized forms.) We should not assume that references to "angels" in the old charms refer to servants of the Christian god. They are simply spirits, with personalities and motivations as varied as the creatures of the natural world. Likewise, the "angels" of the Paternosters are most likely descended from older, pagan spirits, the names and functions of which have shifted over time.

In Celtic traditions, we have the *caim*, which is a kind of spoken prayer that is enunciated as a sphere about the practitioner, positioning them at the center of a consecrated space, my own version of which is as follows:

> *Before me,*
> *Behind me,*
> *Above and below me,*
> *At my right hand,*
> *At my left hand,*
> *I conjure thee, O ring of art.*

We see in this structure the same pattern of directionality, here expressed in a new way, for the magical space around the practitioner actually extends in six directions. Though I call it a "ring" for the sake of tradition, it is really more like a sphere or cube.

In short, what we are after here is a charm that is directionally focused, that positions us in a space that feels different and sacred, but also surrounds us with powerful beings who have some connection to us, either through our land or our cultural heritage, perhaps even through our family.

Your Compass of Art

The tradition of the compass of art is solidly a practice of folk witchery. One of the earliest practical mentions of the witch's compass in print comes from the Scottish witch trials of the 17th and 18th centuries, in which practitioners were believed to "cast a compass" via mysterious ritual, including the words "Here I cast a compass, and there I cast a compass."

Our own compass, then, should be constructed so that it draws on the symbols of our own magical superstitions. These can be determined using certain near-universal associations with the four cardinal directions. We can begin with something simple: the sun rises in the East, and sets in the West. Furthermore, the South is warmer, and the North is colder. (In the southern hemisphere, this is of course reversed.) These basic associations open many possibilities. In terms of seasons, the North would be winter, and the South would be summer. It would make sense for East to be spring (via the dawn, another kind of beginning), and for West to be autumn or fall (sunset, another kind of closure).

We need to call on spirits to attend our compass, but these need not be angels or demons in the ornate hierarchies of the old ceremonial magics. We are folk practitioners, after all, and friendly spirits are all around us already. Simple is always better, so long as it is *meaningful.* Let's look instead to the figures in our own superstitions. What creature, be it animal or plant, is associated with either autumn or the coming of evening in your own superstitions? For many of us, it is the cat, particularly a black cat, and so we can position this creature at the West. The serpent basks in heat, and so it would make sense for it to be associated with the South and its warmth and the season of summer. The hare could make sense in the East, for it proliferates in the spring and is associated with that tide of the year. North is more difficult, for few creatures love the cold, save perhaps the evergreens, like the pine.

Our compass, then, might be conjured with these or similar words:

> *Here I cast this compass mine,*
> *By hare and serpent, cat and pine.*
> *By East and South, by West and North,*
> *Ring of art, I call thee forth.*

We can certainly draw a ring around us while conjuring our compass, as did the sorcerers of old, but we can also simply carve the circle upon the air with our fingers, a convenient modern adaptation. The feeling of the ring carved upon the air should be similar to what you experienced in the magical thread exercise. Perhaps we might light four candles in each of the cardinal directions, or lay a ring of stones or twigs to mark our area. For experienced practitioners, it may be enough to simply form a circle around a single candle using the hands, creating a ring of shadow around the room by the candle's interrupted light. The important thing is that you experience a *feeling* and a *knowing*, that you feel certain beyond all doubt that you are encircled by powerful beings. Developing your own ritual, modeled after the practitioners of old and the hallmarks of your own superstitions, will help you tap into the best source of magical potency: your own roots.

Develop your own compass of art, relying on your own land, culture, and the superstitions thereof. What superstitions did you learn as a child relating to the four directions, about the meaning of the winds (think weather lore), about the rising and setting of the sun? What lore was passed down to you regarding circles? Squares? Consider things that come in groups of four: the seasons, parts of the day (morning, afternoon, evening, night), geographical areas (mountains, meadows, hollows, waters)? Are there four animals that you can think of that are important to the superstitions of your culture? Four plants or trees? What do these old superstitions indicate about the spiritual powers arranged around you?

Clearing Rituals

Rituals used to clear away harmful spiritual presences have been employed throughout magical history, and there are many superstitions surviving to this day that serve this very purpose. The two most popular, whether in the New World or the British Isles, are crossing the fingers and knocking on wood. But spitting, often to the left, is almost as popular a remedy for dark magic or "bad luck" in one's presence. Crossing oneself with the thumb is also quite widespread. Bathing and washing features in a great many old superstitions, often utilizing water from a local, natural source.

To create a simple, workable charm that is our own and connected to our own superstitions, we can turn to an old grimoiric formula:

Asperges me, Domine, hyssopo, et mundabor.
Lavabis me, et supernivem dealbabor.

Asperge me with hyssop, Lord, and I shall be clean.
Wash me, and I shall be whiter than snow.

To "asperge" something means to sprinkle, as in dipping a stalk of hyssop in water, then shaking it about so that droplets land on the intended person. We've no need, however, for hyssop or liturgical language, however interestingly heretical they may be in the context of the old grimoires.

Instead, we can adopt this basic formula to arrive at our own cleansing charm that is rooted in our own unique cultural milieu. What three superstitions can you find, in your own cultural context, that have to do with bathing, washing, or cleansing? I grew up hearing about the first dew of May Day, and how its water could clear the complexion if one woke up early enough. Most of us have heard the superstitions about salt driving away evil. In Scottish tradition, the smoke of smoldering juniper purges evil from a home. Therefore, my own *asperges me* charm might go something like this:

> *Wash me with the waters of May,*
> *and I shall be clean.*
> *Bless me with salt,*
> *and I shall be made whole.*
> *Bathe me in smoke of juniper,*
> *and no evil shall touch me.*

This spoken charm should be combined with actions, perhaps one of the three mentioned: asperging with clean water, or casting salt or salted water, or fumigating oneself with smoke. Whatever actions I select for my ritual should conduct the same sensations we felt in the thread exercise. Again, the important thing is to *feel* any unwanted presence fleeing your person. The words and rituals should evoke this feeling strongly. This is why building your own rituals in your own cultural context will always be more potent than merely following another's instructions.

Consider, then, how you might construct such a cleansing ritual. Go ahead and go for it. Don't worry about the rhymes or the syllables. Focus on including three cleansing superstitions that speak to you, that will conjure for you a true feeling of cleanliness, of readiness, of being unhindered and unbound by any will but your own. What words or actions are associated, in your own superstitions, with cleansing away what is harmful, warding off bad luck and ill omens, and purifying what is unclean? Can you think of plants or animals associated with cleanliness? Can you think of common household ingredients, like salt or clean water? Let these associations guide you to your own old magic, to the magic that is already a part of you, waiting to be realized in fuller form.

One important note, however, about clearing rituals: sometimes, friendly or benign spiritual presences can announce themselves in ways that make us uncomfortable. Before chasing away a spirit who has made himself known to you, consider whether this spirit is really harmful. It's quite rude, after all, to chase a guest from your door without even allowing them to speak. And a friendly spirit can actually *become* a malevolent one if it detects a lack of manners. Many of our surviving faery tales are intended to transmit this very lesson, so that we might avoid angering spirits by accident, making an enemy where there might have been an ally in our craft. The rules of spirit contact need not be any more complex than dealings with your own neighbors, requiring both manners and clear boundaries. Divinatory practices, which we will explore next, can offer a great deal of clarity about the nature of a spiritual presence, allowing us to avoid unnecessary conflict altogether.

Divinatory Rituals

Divination refers, of course, to rituals designed to reveal what is unknown, whether that be the future or simply a more complete, insightful understanding of the present or the past. I highly recommend having a basic divinatory ritual "at the ready" for times when the solution to a problem feels unclear. This can often reveal what sort of charm or working would get at the heart of the problem so that we are not wasting our magical efforts by throwing proverbial darts at a board.

For hundreds of years, folk practitioners have cast bones and coins, drawn runes or ogham, scattered seeds, scried upon flame or water, interpreted dreams, and analyzed the moon and stars. My own practice relies heavily on cartomancy, for there exists a long tradition of card reading that is part of my heritage. (In fact, I wrote a book on the subject.) If you do not have a favorite system of divination already, I highly recommend two simple practices that are adaptable to the culture and taste of any folk witch: sortilege and bibliomancy.

Sortilege is the broad category to which cartomancy and any "drawing of lots" already belongs. It simply means pulling something random from a stack of possibilities and allowing the invisible hand of fate to reveal answers. Every oracle deck for sale in every metaphysical shop is a tool of sortilege. But making your own deck allows you to ruminate on the superstitions and symbols of your own history, designing a deck of cards that speaks to your own magic. To begin this work, make a list of key superstitions related to a very wide variety of subjects. Perhaps a penny heads-up for good financial luck, and a penny heads-down for bad. Perhaps a spider for protection about the home, and a red bird for messages from loved ones. Simplify these images so that you can draw them cleanly. Recreate them with minimal lines and as few details as necessary. Once you are happy with your images, draw them on a blank deck of cards, and you have your very own deck of superstitious sortilege, a magical tool of divination that is yours and yours alone.

Bibliomancy is an even simpler option. It is known in some cultures as "bible-dipping," and the most common form of practice is to take an old family bible and thumb randomly through its pages, allowing a finger to fall on a specific passage. That passage is then interpreted in the context of the question at hand. There is no need, however, to use the bible; any book will do, so long as it is lengthy enough and contains enough breadth in terms of tone and subject. But do choose a book that is meaningful and perhaps sentimental to you; something that smacks of your own story, your own history, something deeply tied to the story of where you come from. (In a pinch, one might use the latter portion of this very book, since its subjects are quite varied and divided into small, self-contained list items.)

Here are a few key tips on divinatory ritual. Treat the entire event as if you were consulting someone whose opinion you respect deeply. If we were meeting with a colleague, for example, we might ask how they are and thank them for taking the time. Show this same respect in your divinatory ritual by lighting a candle and perhaps some incense. If you were meeting with a colleague, you would probably also have questions/topics in mind to guide the conversation. Show this same level of respect in your divinatory ritual by thinking carefully in advance about the question you are going to pose. For answers with depth and detail, focus on "how," "what," or "why" questions instead of "yes" or "no" questions. Give yourself ample time to gaze at the cards or the passage (or what have you) that spells out the answer to your question. Treat it as a kind of contemplative meditation. Don't rush to a single, quick interpretation, but instead, consider multiple possibilities. Perhaps have a journal or a piece of paper nearby to make note of seemingly conflicting or ambiguous messages. In divination, the more seriously you treat these messages, the more layers of meaning will be revealed to you.

Superstitious Charms and Spells

All superstitions, as we have already established, originate in ancient rituals. They are, quite literally, spiritual customs that have stood for so long that their cultural context has been lost and the memory of their meaning has faded. The magical potency that lingers in surviving superstitions can, however, be rekindled. This process is, in truth, a work of *reconsecration*, for we are stoking once again the sacred flame in the charm that has dwindled down to embers. There are many ways to do this, depending on the witch's needs and the situation at hand:

Direct derivation is the most straightforward approach. The actions of the superstition are undertaken intentionally in a ritual context. Example: The witch wishes to experience relief from some old emotional pain, and so she casts her compass, then takes up a handful of salt. She clenches the salt in her fists, focusing all of her pain into it, chanting, *I conjure thee, o creature of salt, to absorb this pain, and take it from me.* The salt is then cast away, most likely on a place far from the witch's home so that the pain does not come back. In this working, the witch uses a fairly direct interpretation of the old superstition that clenching salt in one's fists relieves pain.

Indirect derivation can be more complex and creative. In this approach, one or more elements of the superstition are adapted, with new elements added based on the witch's needs and intuition. Example: The witch consecrates a charm bag filled with salt and soothing herbs for a friend suffering from chronic pain. She instructs them to keep it on their person to help manage the pain. This working is a new interpretation of the same superstition, here paired with some herbal knowledge, and adapted into a charm bag that can be given to the intended party as a talisman.

Inverse derivation is occasionally useful, as it allows us to accomplish the reversed outcome indicated by the superstition itself. In this approach, the superstition's normal sequence is set backwards and revised with various added elements in order to bring the opposite effect. Example: the witch consecrates a cursing powder made with salt and saturnine herbs, filling it with pain and suffering, then places it somewhere the enemy will spill it. The original superstition indicates only that salt mitigates pain, but the clever witch has toyed with this formula, using salt as a *conduit* for pain, to direct its course of movement in order to transfer pain from one party to another. When the enemy spills the salt, they are releasing it, and the charm is complete.

Ominous derivation is perhaps the most familiar form of superstitious observance. Simply put, the elements of the superstition are read as an omen or portent, either directly or in the interpretation of related words or images appearing in dreams, divinations, or visionary experiences. Example: the witch dreams of holding salt, and interprets that suffering may be on its way, but can be subverted with the appropriate magical approach. If the witch is wise, she would turn to a cleansing charm in this moment in order to subvert the ill omen. Remember that fate is never written in stone. All dark portents can be cast off with the right magical approach, for nothing in the future is fixed.

Festivals and Days

One section of this book is devoted purely to superstitions pertaining to special days and festivals, and for good reason. Certain charms, according to generations past, were more effective at certain points in the seasonal cycle. All Hallows' Eve, for example, is an auspicious night for divination, spirit contact, and warding. The first morning of May, in some folk traditions, is an auspicious time for charms of beauty, health, and success.

Consider, in your own context, what superstitions survive regarding the importance of days and times. How might these old seasonal customs lend themselves to magical rituals? Often with such rites, the goal is twofold: to honor, in some way, the inherent nature of the season at hand, and to accomplish some practical magical goal that is aligned with that current. And so part of this work is understanding the personality of the season itself, what workings it lends itself to naturally, and what spiritual forces may be tucked away neatly in the superstition that has survived to this day.

Some of the old festival customs come with stories worth preserving, for they reveal another layer of meaning to a charm that feels simple and plain. The Irish tale of Stingy Jack and the Devil, for instance, is deeply connected to the tradition of the jack-o-lantern, just as the old lore of the evergreens is connected to the modern Christmas tree. You may wish to develop your own version of several folktales, something that can be remembered during these seasons, and this will strengthen and vivify the threads of tradition that are, if you recall, the backbone of practical folk witchery.

On Heretical Instruments

Many student witches begin the work of developing their own folk practice, only to be appalled and affronted by the use of liturgy, biblical passages, and mentions of the saints in the magic of their ancestors. For some, this barrier is insurmountable, especially if they have experienced trauma at the hands of the church, a sadly common event for many people, but especially for women and queer and trans practitioners. Feelings of sexual shame, rejection, judgment, and manipulation are painful, and these feelings can be triggered by symbols that remind us of abusive encounters with religious people from the past.

These feelings are valid, and I will not minimize them. I can only speak for myself and my own craft when I say that, while I do practice charms with liturgical language, I am not a Christian. I do not worship the Christian god, and I do not follow Christ. It is not my goal to live out my afterlife in the Christian heaven; I have no desire to be a child in that kingdom, under the rule of that god. This is not a barb against the believers, only a statement of fact. From what I have read of that god, we don't quite see eye-to-eye, so I don't think his heaven would be a good fit, really. An uncomfortable arrangement, at best. But for all of eternity. And with a lot of singing, they say.

My craft, like the craft of my ancestors, involves borrowing from potent magical symbols, threads that have become strong through repetition and mass belief, and yes, some of those threads come from the church. They do not *originate* in the church, of course, but they have been used by the church for so long that the association is plain to see. When I draw on these threads in the practice of witchcraft, I am twisting and braiding them to my own ends, to serve my own defined goals. To put it simply, I'm neither a Christian nor a Satanist, but a practical folk witch, drawing on what is useful and connected to my traditions. This approach is sometimes called *heretical* craft, but don't let that scare you. After all, Joan of Arc and Queen Elizabeth I were both called heretics in their day.

This approach is sometimes likened to a serpent's path, weaving back and forth between holiness and unholiness, dextral and sinistral, the right-hand path and the left-hand path—and so, the old forms of traditional witchery are sometimes called "the crooked path." There is, at the heart of folk witchery, an inherent irony, a delicious contrast that is heretical in nature, like a riddle woven into the core of our magics. For me, this feels less like a back-and-forth, and more like a very natural, inherent mixture. Like a whiskey that is flavored by the wooden barrels in which it has rested for some time. You may taste the oak, but that isn't the real point, is it? After all, if it didn't get you drunk, you would never drink something that tasted like oak. But perhaps your parents made whiskey in those barrels, and their parents before them, and their parents before them. And so, when you taste the oak, you remember. It feels familiar and nostalgic, and it gets the job done. The point is that *feeling* and *belonging*, not the oak itself. Likewise, liturgical charms are really about *tradition*, not *religion*.

It is important to acknowledge that none of this is new. The witch hunts in Scotland were driven, in large part, by a vehement opposition to the mingling of Christianity and paganism. The old heretical magics wrested power away from religious authorities and placed it firmly in the hands of healers, charmers, and skilly folk, to use for blessing friends and cursing enemies alike, according to their own needs. The protestant movement was, in many ways, about creating a new form of Christianity that was purged of all the old pagan, magical elements that had been woven into it over hundreds of years. And so, the heretical element of modern folk witchery is not a new "angle" or subversive "trend," but a continuation. It is an acknowledgement of a complex relationship with the church that is deeply historical and very much pagan.

If you are new to folk witchery and feel overwhelmed by all of this, my advice to you is simple: just don't worry about it, at least in the beginning. Focus on where you come from, on what grounds you, on what feels warm and familiar and empowering. Focus on who you are. Don't worry about being mislabeled as a Satanist witch or a Christian witch or whatever. Don't agonize over whether you should call yourself this sort of witch or that sort of witch. It doesn't actually matter how other people see your practice; being understood won't help you build your craft or connect with spirits or excel in your charm-work. Being understood is highly overrated, because the easiest sort of person to understand *is a dullard*. Instead, I encourage you to be the complex, messy, enigmatic, sorcerous creature that you already are. Don't reduce yourself. Don't make yourself dull. Don't file down your edges; sharpen them until they gleam, like silver in the moonlight. Such cutlery will serve you well someday, and years from now, you will look back and be thankful that you did not blunt such brilliant instruments, that you did not diminish the authentic, unique magical mixture that lies at the core of you.

Superstitions of Birth, Family, & Home

- Discarded eggshells, if left unbroken, will be used by witches as boats to sail at sea. (Widespread, British Isles & New World.)
- To break a mirror brings seven years bad luck, unless that mirror be buried shortly after. (Widespread, British Isles & New World.)
- To keep a child's caul preserved and stored in the house brings good luck. (Widespread, British Isles & New World.)

- To drop a fork signifies that a man will arrive at one's home. (Widespread, British Isles & New World.)
- To drop a knife signifies that a woman will arrive at one's home. (Widespread, British Isles & New World.)
- To drop a serving spoon signifies that a widow will arrive at one's home. (Widespread, British Isles & New World.)
- A person who cuts bread into thick slices will become a good parent. (Widespread, British Isles.)
- It is good luck to steal a dishcloth from one's neighbor. (Widespread, British Isles & New World.)
- The month in which a child is born will denote their qualities thusly (Widespread, British Isles & New World.):

-January: Industrious and hard-working.

-February: Loves money much, but romance more.

-March: Honest and rather handsome.

-April: Maladies and danger when traveling.

-May: Handsome and amiable.

-June: Small of stature and very fond of children.

-July: Fat and loyal.

-August: Ambitious and courageous.

-September: Strong and prudent.

-October: Wicked and inconstant, with a florid complexion.

-November: Happy, but untrustworthy.

-December: Passionate and charitable.

♦ The day on which a child is born will denote their qualities (Widespread, British Isles & New World.):

> *Monday's child is fair of face.*
> *Tuesday's child is full of grace.*
> *Wednesday's child is full of woe.*
> *Thursday's child has far to go.*
> *Friday's child is loving and giving.*
> *Saturday's child works hard for a living.*
> *But the child which is born on the Sabbath day*
> *Is blythe and bonnie, and good and gay.*

♦ The month in which one is born denotes one's lucky stone (Widespread, British Isles & New World.):

> *By those in January born,*
> *No gem save Garnets should be worn;*
> *They will ensure your constancy,*
> *True friendship and fidelity.*
>
> *The February born will find*
> *Sincerity and peace of mind,*
> *Freedom from passion and from care*
> *If they the Amethyst will wear.*

Who in this world of ours their eyes
In March first opens, shall be wise;
In days of peril, firm and brave,
And wear a Bloodstone to their grave.

Those who in April date their years,
Diamonds shall wear, lest bitter tears
For vain repentance flow. This stone
Emblem of innocence is known.

Who first beholds the light of day
In Spring's sweet flowery month of May,
And wears the Emerald all her life,
Shall be a loved and happy wife.

Who comes with summer to this earth,
And owes to June her day of birth,
With ring of Agate on her hand,
Can health, wealth, and peace command.

The glowing Ruby should adorn
Those who in warm July are born;
Thus will they be exempt and free
From love's doubts and anxiety.

Wear a Sardonyx, or for thee
No conjugal felicity.
The August born without this stone
'Tis said must live unloved alone.

A maiden born when Autumn's leaves
Are rustling in September's breeze,
A Sapphire on her brow should bind,
'Twill cure diseases of the mind.

October's child is full of woe,
And life's vicissitudes must know;
But lay an Opal on her breast,
And hope will lull her woes to rest.

Who first comes to this world below
With dull November's fog and snow,
Should prize the Topaz' amber hue,
Emblem of friends and lovers true.

If cold December gave you birth,
The month of snow and ice and mirth,
Place on your hand the Turquoise blue,
Success will bless you if you do.

◆ The month in which one is born denotes one's guardian angel or spirit (Widespread, British Isles & New World.):

-January is the month of Gabriel, who brings consolation and constancy.

-February is the month of Barchiel, who guards youths and checks one's passions.

-March is the month of Malchidiel, who brings power and defense in times of need.

-April is the month of Ashmodel, who is wise and offers sound guidance.

-May is the month of Amriel, who brings hope and a full share of blessings.

-June is the month of Muriel, who gives a long life of luxury and ease.

-July is the month of Verchiel, who brings eloquence and defends against enemies.

-August is the month of Hamatiel, who guards against betrayal.

-September is the month of Tsuriel, who protects against worries and brings happiness.

-October is the month of Bariel, who protects against injustice and misfortune.

> *-November is the month of Adnachiel, who sends wise and loyal friends.*
> *-December is the month of Humiel, who brings success and happiness.*

- To spill salt is unlucky. (Widespread, British Isles & New World.)
- Eggshells are used by witches in order to sink boats by floating the shells on the surface of a bowl of water, then upsetting the surface to make them sink. (Widespread, British Isles.)
- If a woman wears dock seeds on her left arm, she is sure to become pregnant. (Ireland.)
- If an infant is given three drops of water to drink just before it is baptized, it will speak three truths in response to any questions. (Ireland.)
- When cooking, stir with a fork, and you stir up sorrow. (Ireland.)
- The breaking of a corkscrew is an omen of long-lasting, dire poverty. (England.)
- The manner in which a candle burns indicates possible futures (England):

> -A flying bit of glowing ash: a letter arriving soon.
> -A brightly glowing wick: a sweetheart.
> -An ashen thread from the wick falling: a thief.
> -A curl of wax down the side: a death shroud.
> -A blue flaa ghost nearby.

- A slice of bacon shared between two brings a year of happiness. (England.)
- If one gives a knife to another as a gift, something must be exchanged in return, otherwise the thread between them is cut. (England.)
- To step over a broom handle brings on pregnancy. (England.)
- To break a mirror is to lose a friend. (England.)
- If you wish to remember something, tie a knot in a handkerchief. (England.)
- To give a pin brings bad luck to the giver. The provider of the pin should stipulate that the other party is taking it, not being gifted it. (England.)
- To cut a cross into a rising loaf of bread confers blessings upon it, and wards off evil. (England.)
- A loaf of bread with a large empty cavern of air in the middle is an ill omen. (England.)
- A father's hat, hung on his child's bedpost, will ward away wicked spirits. (Scotland.)
- Walking backwards sets a curse on one's parents. (New World.)
- One water witch (a person who can divine water by the use of dowsing rods) is born in each family. (New World.)
- The seventh son of a seventh son will be a charmer. (New World.)
- A child who steps on all of his books will never miss a lesson. (New World.)

- Hide mirrors from babies to ease teething. (New World).
- Place a child on the floor with a bible, a dollar bill, and a deck of cards. The one she chooses will indicate her profession. The bible indicates learning or religion. The dollar bill indicates business and finances. The deck of cards indicates a scoundrel. (New World.)
- To keep away company when none is desired, take a used dishcloth and shake it, and you will shake off the intended visitors. (New World.)
- To kiss a new baby brings good luck. (New World.)
- Whoever possesses a child's afterbirth controls their fate for good or ill. (New World.)
- A child born with a veil will be able to see the future. (New World.)
- If a child has long, thick hair, it will not grow healthy, for its strength will have gone into its hair. (New World.)
- A new baby carried up the stairs will rise in the world. (New World.)
- If a child sleeps with a book under its pillow, it will have learned the lesson the next day. (New World.)
- A nose itch when one is away from home means you are missed at home. (New World.)
- One should not enter a new home without salt. (New World.)
- If you place a lock of someone's hair under your doorstep, they will be unable to stay away. (New World.)

- Cutting a new door in an old house brings a death in the family. (New World.)
- If one forgets to wash a skillet, an unexpected guest will show up for the next meal. (New World.)
- If everything is eaten at a meal, the next day will have fine weather. (New World.)
- If thirteen people sit down to share a meal, one will die within a month. (New World.)
- If two forks are placed beside one's plate, one will attend either a wedding or a funeral. (New World.)
- If you walk without stepping on any cracks in pavement, you will have a good supper. (New World.)
- Early to bed and early to rise makes one healthy, wealthy, witty, and wise. (New World.)
- To climb over anyone in bed brings bad luck. (New World.)
- When placing shoes or slippers under the bed, place them toes out in order to bring good luck. (New World.)
- The head of one's bed should point North in order to bring good luck. (New World.)

Superstitions of Love & Marriage

- To be blessed with good health throughout a marriage, set the bed on the wedding night so that the head of the bed points to the rising sun. (Widespread, British Isles & New World.)
- To interrupt the making of the marriage bed causes sorrow to the couple. (Widespread, British Isles & New World.)

- To cause the bride to have a troubled life and an unhappy marriage, trick her into drinking some vinegar on her wedding day. (Widespread, British Isles & New World.)

- You may divine whether someone loves you by picking the petals of a flower, saying "s/he loves me; s/he loves me not" for each petal. The final petal indicates which of the statements is true. (Widespread, British Isles & New World.)

- To spill wine on the bride's wedding dress will cause bloodshed in the family within a year. (Widespread, British Isles & New World.)

- If a pigeon flies and lands on the church before the couple walk in to be married, it is a sign of good fortune for their future life together. (Widespread, British Isles & New World.)

- Consult the last chapter of Proverbs to determine what sort of husband or wife someone will be. The day of the month on which they were born indicates the appropriate passage to read. (Widespread, British Isles & New World.)

- To wear the color red to a wedding brings bad luck to the marriage. (Widespread, British Isles & New World.)

- To obtain a lock of your beloved's hair and keep it next to your heart will cause them to love you in return. (Widespread, British Isles & New World.)

- Different kinds of kisses signify different sorts of love in store for a couple. (Widespread, British Isles & New World.)

-A kiss on the forehead signifies respect for intellect.

-A kiss on the cheek signifies admiration for beauty.

-A kiss on the nose signifies awkwardness, or appreciation for humor.

-A kiss on the chin signifies admiration for one who is "above" you.

-A kiss on the hand signifies timidity and homage.

-A kiss on the lips signifies love.

-A short kiss signifies carelessness.

-A long kiss signifies passionate devotion.

- To hide a horseshoe behind the flowers hung up in the church during a wedding will bring good fortune to the bride. (Widespread, British Isles.)

- There should be no buttonhole unfastened on either the bride or groom, or else wicked faeries will enter through the hole and steal away their heart. (Widespread, British Isles.)

- The Dumb Cake can predict a future love, and it should be made thus: two persons must mix the batter, two must bake it, and two must slice it. A third person should then place a slice under the pillows of all three. All of this must be done without speaking a word. All parties will then dream that night of their future sweethearts. (Widespread, British Isles.)

- Go at night and pull up some kale without looking. Its health and shape will denote the qualities of your future mate. Soil clinging to the roots indicates wealth. (Scotland.)

- If the ale drunk at a marriage is well-fermented and strong, this signifies good fortune for the newlywed couple. (Scotland.)

- It is unlucky for a new bride to be the first person to enter an empty home after her wedding. (Scotland.)

- If a young woman wishes to know who her future husband will be, let her go alone to a darkened room and gaze into a mirror set to reflect the moonlight while eating an apple. Her true love's face will appear in the mirror. (Scotland.)

- A man or woman with a beauty mark can compel love from anyone they desire. (Scotland.)

- Write the names of several unmarried couples on holly twigs, tied together with thread so that there are several pairs arranged in a circle, then set a hot coal in the middle. The pair to catch fire first will be wed, but one must call aloud to the husband to "quench the fire, in the name of the Devil" for it to come to pass. (Ireland.)

- To ensure a lover's fidelity, place a pinch of cumin into their food or drink. (Ireland.)

- A posset eaten by the groom on the wedding night will make the man both kind and virile. (England.)

- To dream of your future spouse, stand upon something you have never stood on before, holding kale in your hand, and drink something nine times, then go to bed backwards. (England.)

- To allow a hen to enter the home of a newlywed couple and cluck about noisily will bring good luck to the household. (England.)

- If a jilted lover wishes to curse their former sweetheart's new marriage, they have only to attend the wedding and cast a handful of rue at the couple. (England.)

- It is lucky for the bride to be married with a pinch of salt in her pocket. (Isle of Man.)

- If a young woman asks the new moon to show reveal her future husband, it will do so in her dreams. This must be done standing in the open air, for the moon will ignore prayers made through window glass. (Isle of Man.)

- After a couple is wed, the first one to drink from a well will become the master of the house in all things, and the other will do their will. (Cornwall.)

- If a young woman would know what sort of husband she shall have, she should go to a wood pile after dark and draw out a stick without light to see. Its form will determine her husband's nature. A straight and even stick indicates a loving, kind husband. A twisted, knotty, or crooked stick indicates a foul-tempered, unlikeable sort. (New World.)

- If a young woman wishes to see her love's face, let her go to an old well at midnight, and into it cast two kernels of corn. She must then call to her husband and hold a mirror over the well so that it reflects the dark water below. She will see her true love's face in the mirror. (New World.)

- To estrange two lovers from one another, cast graveyard dirt between them. (New World.)

- Light a candle at midnight, then prick it three times with a needle while saying the name of either a loved one or an enemy, along with the words "Thrice the candle pricked by me; Thrice thy heart shall broken be." If you name a loved one, and they betray you, their heart will be broken three times in return. If you name an enemy, they will love three times in vain. (New World.)

- To have lines in the palm of one's hand spelling the letter M indicates that one will marry rich. (New World.)

- To have a vision of your future mate, go to an abandoned house at midnight and light a candle, then warm a pin in its flame and stick it into the candle's wax. When the pin falls out, a vision of your true love will appear. (New World.)

- If you see a red bird, name the one you wish to love you, and blow a kiss to the bird, and it will ensure that your love comes to pass. (New World.)

- If you can tie some vine into a lover's knot, you can compel anyone you desire to love you in return. (New World.)

- In an empty house, drop a ball of yarn, and wind it as you walk about the house, saying as you do so, "I wind; who holds?" Before the ball is wound up again you will have a vision or some sort of sign of your future mate. (New World.)

- Wearing a sprig of yarrow brings love. (New World.)

- You can compel any person to fall in love with you through the following rather macabre procedure. Catch a toad, and weigh it down under a rock until it perishes. Then dry the toad thoroughly, and grind its remains to a fine powder. Sprinkle this powder on the person you wish to love you. (New World.)

♦ If you can blow all the seeds from a head of thistle, your sweetheart loves you truly. (New World.)

♦ A group of young people may divine their future spouses through the operation called the "Silent Supper" or "Dumb Supper." They must make a fire and prepare a meal together, without speaking, and always moving backwards. A pan of water is set near the door, and a towel or cloth hung nearby. They must sit at the table, but not eat anything, and in doing so, they will receive visions or signs of their future mates, either in the evening or during dreams later that night. (New World.)

♦ A spider appearing on one's neck indicates a secret lover. (New World.)

♦ To see two snakes at once is a sign of a wedding soon. (New World.)

♦ When two beloveds are walking side by side, they should avoid walking through anything that should pass between them, lest this spell division. This influence can be mitigated by saying "bread and butter." (New World.)

Superstitions of the Human Body

- A twitch in the left eye indicates misfortune. (Widespread, British Isles & New World.)
- A twitch in the right eye signifies news coming your way. (Widespread, British Isles & New World.)
- Thin or small eyebrows indicate a weak-minded, superficial person who cannot be relied upon. (Widespread, British Isles & New World.)

- Woolly or bushy eyebrows indicate an angry, fretful, jealous person who is easily provoked to rage. (Widespread, British Isles & New World.)

- White specks on the fingernails indicate various possible futures, depending on which fingernail they be found on, as in the following rhyme, which is counted out upon the fingers (Widespread, British Isles & New World):

  > *A gift* (thumb),
  > *A friend* (index),
  > *A foe* (middle),
  > *A lover to come* (ring),
  > *A journey to go* (pinkie).

- Heavy, arched eyebrows indicate sound judgment and powers of perception. (Widespread, British Isles & New World.)

- Take a fallen eyelash on one finger, and make a wish while blowing it away. It will come true. (Widespread, British Isles & New World.)

- If one wishes for long, shaggy hair, have it cut under the sign of Leo; if one wishes for curly hair, cut it under the sign of Aries. (Widespread, British Isles & New World.)

- To singe one's hair by accident indicates sickness soon to follow. (Widespread, British Isles & New World.)

- The day on which one cuts one's nails can confer different blessings or curses (Widespread, British Isles & New World.):

  > *Cut on Monday, hear good news;*
  > *Cut on Tuesday, get new shoes;*
  > *Cut on Wednesday, cut for wealth;*
  > *Cut on Thursday, cut for health;*
  > *Cut on Friday, cut for woe;*
  > *Cut on Saturday, journey to go;*
  > *Cut on Sunday, cut for evil,*
  > *All next week you'll catch the Devil.*

- To cut one's hair on Good Friday brings excellent luck. (Widespread, British Isles.)
- A ringing in the ears indicates bad news on the way. (Widespread, British Isles.)
- If one hears a ringing in the ears, ask the nearest person for a number between 1 and 26. The letter corresponding to that number indicates the first letter of a word with bearing on the future, often the name of a future spouse. (Widespread, British Isles.)
- A sore, bite, or wound on one's tongue indicates that one has been telling lies. (Widespread, British Isles.)
- The placement of a birthmark indicates both one's qualities and one's future (Widespread, British Isles.):

-A birthmark on or near the nose indicates future wealth and success.

-A birthmark near the eyes indicates trustworthiness and a quiet nature.

-A birthmark on the right side of the forehead indicates a person who will be powerful and celebrated.

-A birthmark on the left side of the forehead indicates a person who will meet with failure.

-A birthmark over the heart indicates a bloody death.

* It brings ill luck to cut your hair or nails on a Friday or a Sunday. (England.)
* The widow's peak indicates that one will outlive their spouse. (England.)
* It brings ill luck to cut your hair on a Monday. (Ireland.)
* Cut hair should be buried rather than burned, for the resurrected dead may go looking for it. (Ireland.)
* After having one's hair cut, all of the clippings should be placed on a fire in order to divine the body's health. If the clippings do not catch flame, this is an ill omen. (Wales.)
* To ease labor, place two crossed hazel twigs upon an open bible, and place this under the pillow. (New World).
* Salt clenched in one's fists can ease labor pains. (New World.)
* An itch on the nose indicates that a visitor will soon arrive. (New World.)

- An itch on the right side of your nose indicates that a loved one is coming. (New World.)
- An itch on the left side of the nose indicates that an enemy is coming. (New World.)
- An itch on the right palm indicates that one will spend money. (New World.)
- An itch on the left palm indicates that one will receive money. (New World.)
- An itch on the foot indicates that one will travel. (New World.)
- An itch on the right food indicates traveling somewhere new. (New World.)
- An itch on the left foot indicates that you will travel where you are unwelcome. (New World.)
- If your left ear itches or burns, someone is speaking ill of you. (New World.)
- If your right ear itches or burns, someone is speaking well of you. (New World.)
- If your right eye itches, you will see something pleasant. (New World.)
- If your left eye itches, you will have excellent luck. (New World.)
- A stye on one's eye indicates one has been telling lies. (New World.)
- A talisman made to resemble a small hand with fingers clenched, either made of coral or black stone, will keep away the evil eye. (New World.)

- Comb your hair at night, and you will dream of the Devil. (New World.)
- A left-handed person owes three days of work to the Devil. (New World.)
- Wash a wart in stump water, and it will vanish by the time the water is gone. (New World.)
- To remove a wart, rub an apple on it, then bury it in secret, saying, "As this apple decays, let my wart go away." (New World.)
- To remove a wart, rub it under the new moon, saying, "You will grow, and you will go," and it will disappear as the moon waxes to full. (New World.)

Superstitions of Money & Success

- Toss a coin into a fountain, and make a wish. Your wish will come true. (Widespread, British Isles & New World.)
- It is lucky, when beginning a new undertaking, to give alms or charity, as this will ensure success in the new endeavors. (Widespread, British Isles & New World.)

- Any new business should be begun on the new moon, so that it will wax with the moon's growth. (Widespread, British Isles & New World.)

- The luckiest day for business or financial dealings is the day of the week on which you were born. (Widespread, British Isles & New World.)

- It is lucky to have a fat person about when conducting business. (Widespread, British Isles & New World.)

- To find a darning needle just before making an exchange or a purchase brings good luck. (Widespread, British Isles & New World.)

- It is unlucky to finalize any business dealings on a Sunday. (Widespread, British Isles & New World.)

- To step over straw will foil a new enterprise. (Widespread, British Isles & New World.)

- Always carry "seed money" in your pocket; that is, money that will grow and attract more money. (Widespread, British Isles & New World.)

- Keep the first new coin that comes to you in the new year, and it will bring you prosperity throughout the whole rest of the year to come. (Widespread, British Isles & New World.)

- To see a spider indicates luck in a new enterprise. (Widespread, British Isles & New World.)

- One who buries money must wander around after their death until it is found. (Widespread, British Isles & New World.)

♦ The day on which one invests money or gives money to a friend starting a new venture of any kind determines the fate soon to come (Widespread, British Isles & New World.):

> -On Monday, you will make a promise, but not fulfill it.
> -On Tuesday, you will ruin your fortune by needless delay.
> -On Wednesday, you will soon change your present abode.
> -On Thursday, something unpleasant is preparing for you.
> -On Friday, unhappy in love, but fortunate in other respects.
> -On Saturday, a hasty quarrel through a trifle.

♦ To win against any lawsuit, wear some lard on your person, so that you slip from the enemy's grip. (Widespread, British Isles & New World.)

♦ Money dropped when one person passes it to another signifies that more money will be exchanged between them over future dealings. (Widespread, British Isles & New World.)

♦ To change a run of ill luck in your finances, stand under the new moon in the open air, and rub your purse or wallet while gazing at the moon, saying "What I rub and what I see, both alike increase for me." Take care, though, not to let the new moon see the inside of an empty purse or wallet, lest the moon bring you more of nothing. (Widespread, British Isles & New World.)

- Money received as a gift should be spat upon for good luck. (Widespread, British Isles.)

- The first money received for a business transaction in a day should be spat upon before putting it away, so that it brings more money to follow. (Widespread, British Isles.)

- When making a bargain or exchange of any sort, a coin should be given by one party to the other in order to bring both parties luck and satisfaction from the deal. (England.)

- When building or repairing a home, fix coins into the cob or concrete. These hidden coins will attract more money to the family who resides there. (Ireland.)

- To die with money hidden from relatives brings bad luck to the entire family. (Wales.)

- It is unlucky to report anyone to the police for crimes of petty theft. (Scotland.)

- To find a penny heads-up spells luck in one's finances. (New World.)

- To find a penny heads-down spells money trouble. To mitigate the ill luck, do not pick it up. (New World.)

- To carry an old coin in one's pocket brings good luck. (New World.)

- If the initials of your name can be used to spell a word, you are destined for wealth. (New World.)

♦ A two-dollar bill brings ill luck to the receiver. Avert this ill luck by tearing off a little piece of the side, but not from the corner. (New World.)

♦ To find a piece of silver brings excellent luck. (New World.)

♦ If you find money lying anywhere, be sure to keep it, for it will bring more money your way. (New World.)

♦ Drop a nickel on an old, wooden floor. If it lands between boards and sticks straight up, you will have excellent luck. (New World.)

♦ Bury a coin somewhere when you are young, and by the time you are grown, you will have riches. (New World.)

♦ The day on which you pay your rent indicates one of several futures (New World.):

    -On Sunday, signifies a journey for business.

    -On Monday, that you will shortly be much pleased.

    -On Tuesday, that you will have luck in preventing a loss.

    -On Wednesday, a speedy recovery.

    -On Thursday, success in one's undertakings.

    -On Friday, to become public and notorious.

    -On Saturday, the death of the last person you kissed.

♦ Take the first piece of money you receive in the morning, and place it in your stocking, and you will get more. (New World.)

♦ Hide money in the foundation of a new building as it is being built, and you will have great luck. (New World.)

+ A silver dollar found and kept will bring great wealth and fortune. (New World.)
+ Paper money folded lengthwise ensures that more money will come to you. (New World.)
+ Paper money folded short-ways ensures that one will lose money. (New World.)
+ To see a lizard brings good fortune in one's finances. (New World.)
+ The day of the week on which you withdraw money from the bank indicates one of several possible futures (New World.):

> -On Monday, signifies a great loss and severely felt.
> -On Tuesday, that you will soon fall sick, but recover quickly.
> -On Wednesday, that you will soon discern friends from foes.
> -On Thursday, that you will gain a happy establishment.
> -On Friday, long life, happiness, riches and contentment.
> -On Saturday, that you will soon form a lasting attachment.

+ Carry a piece of oyster shell in your pocket, and you will someday have riches. (New World.)

Superstitions of Travel & Journeys

- To begin a journey with the right foot brings good luck for the road ahead. (Widespread, British Isles & New World.)
- To begin a journey with the left foot brings trouble on the road ahead. (Widespread, British Isles & New World.)
- To be late for one's transportation foretells quarrels on the road ahead. (Widespread, British Isles & New World.)

♦ To sit backwards in a railroad car brings bad luck. (Widespread, British Isles & New World.)

♦ If you find money on a railroad track or a well-traveled road, it indicates that you will go on a journey soon. (Widespread, British Isles & New World.)

♦ To break a watch indicates that you will travel. (Widespread, British Isles & New World.)

♦ A scar on the right hand indicates that one will travel and see the world. (Widespread, British Isles & New World.)

♦ If one's windows fog with steam, and water runs down them in lines, it indicates a journey soon by water. (Widespread, British Isles & New World.)

♦ To dream of oneself walking can suggest various futures, depending on the manner (Widespread, British Isles & New World):

-Walking alone, slowly: Sadness and poverty

-Walking fast: Success or anxiety in pursuit of a goal

-Walking through fire: Danger

-Walking with another: Comfort and friendship

-Walking with a younger person: Marriage

-Walking and smiling: Success, joy, prosperity

♦ If a conductor asks for your fare twice, you will have a troubled journey. (Widespread, British Isles & New World.)

- To sweep the floor immediately after a visitor leaves brings them ill luck on the road. (Widespread, British Isles & New World.)
- When a ship is departing with many passengers, it is good luck for one of their loved ones to take off one shoe and throw it after the vessel as it sails away. (Widespread, British Isles & New World.)
- To walk over a newly poured sidewalk without speaking ensures success for a year. (Widespread, British Isles & New World.)
- If one has a mark going across the nose, they will wander across many lands. (Widespread, British Isles & New World.)
- If, as you are traveling about, you encounter a funeral procession and hear a dog barking, do not look at the dog. If you do, it may bring sickness your way. (Widespread, British Isles & New World.)
- The seventh floor of a hotel brings ill luck. (Widespread, British Isles & New World.)
- A rider with a sprig of boxwood attached to his horse will have excellent fortune. (Widespread, British Isles.)
- A whip with an adder's tongue braided into its leather will ensure healthy, obedient horses. (Widespread, British Isles.)
- If one sets out in the morning and encounters a person whose face they do not like, they should turn back and begin the journey again in order to have good luck for the day. (Scotland.)
- Before embarking on any travels, borrow money from a woman, and you will have good luck. (New World.)

- If you set off somewhere, but are forced to return three times in a row, you will have trouble on the road ahead. (New World.)
- The following hotel rooms are considered lucky: 9, 18, 27, 36, 45, 63, 72, 81, 90, 109, 207, 306, 405, 504, 603, 702, 801, 900. (New World.)
- If you attempt to travel somewhere with wet clothes in tow, you will have bad luck. (New World.)
- For two women to kiss one another on the street brings ill luck. (New World.)
- It brings bad luck to kick an old shoe that you find lying on the sidewalk. (New World.)
- To see four ladies walking together is a sign of excellent luck, unless you are one of the ladies. (New World.)
- To go riding about in the moonlight foretells domestic troubles. (New World.)
- To dream of oneself walking aimlessly down the street foretells the arrival of troubles and worries. (New World.)
- For good luck and safety while traveling, it is good luck to sit with the feet crossed. (New World.)
- Every hotel has one room in it that brings bad luck. (New World.)
- It brings good luck and protection from evil to set a horseshoe on a train's cow catcher. (New World.)
- To encounter the same person when embarking on a trip and when returning home brings good fortune. (New World.)
- To see a yellow box-car brings good luck. (New World.)

- It brings excellent luck to cross a street from corner to corner, repeating the words "bread and butter" three times in a row. (New World.)

- If you take off your shoes casually, and they call in the form of a cross, it indicates a journey in your future. (New World.)

- If you are embraced by someone you do not recognize, you will travel far. (New World.)

- If, while traveling, you take a table at a restaurant and are brought a torn napkin, you will have a prosperous and successful journey. (New World.)

- If a car breaks down while going downhill, it foretells a death. (New World.)

Superstitions of Plants & Trees

- Anoint the body with chicory before asking a great favor, and it cannot be refused. (Widespread, British Isles & New World.)
- Ash trees, and the wood thereof, may attract lightning during a storm, as in the saying, "avoid an ash; it counts the flash." (Widespread, British Isles & New World.)

♦ The oak tree and its wood is said to attract lightning bolts, as in the saying, "beware of an oak; it draws the stroke." (Widespread, British Isles & New World.)

♦ Thorny trees, such as the blackthorn and whitethorn, are said to be an excellent defense against lightning and other forms of harm, as in the saying, "creep under the thorn; it can save you from harm." (Widespread, British Isles & New World.)

♦ The whitethorn tree gave the thorns that made Christ's crown, and so it was blessed with powers of protection to this day. (Widespread, British Isles & New World.)

♦ A cross made of the twigs of the hazel tree can heal the bite of an adder and many other ailments besides. (Widespread, British Isles & New World.)

♦ When a beekeeper wants to attract a new colony of bees to take up residence in an empty hive, he should place the hive near the plant called melissa, or else smear the leaves on the hive, for bees cannot resist it. (Widespread, British Isles & New World.)

♦ Blow all of the tufted seeds from a dandelion head (or, variously, a thistle head), and your wish will come true. (Widespread, British Isles & New World.)

♦ Cinquefoil's five petals denote the five wounds of Christ. It brings honor and mastery in all things. (Widespread, British Isles & New World.)

♦ Fleabane repels unwanted pests. (Widespread, British Isles & New World.)

- St. John's wort protects against the machinations of dark sorcery. (Widespread, British Isles & New World.)
- The spear-shaped leaves of the mugwort plant protect against harm, especially from wicked spirits and black magic. (Widespread, British Isles & New World.)
- John the Baptist, when he wandered about the wilderness, wore a girdle of mugwort about himself, and so to this day, the plant protects from evil. (Widespread, British Isles & New World.)
- Break the seed-pouch of a shepherd's purse, and you will break a heart. (Widespread, British Isles & New World.)
- Take a poppy pod, and make a hole in it, emptying out all of the seeds. Write your question on a small tear of paper, and roll it tightly so that it fits inside the pod. Place the poppy pod under your pillow before sleeping at night, saying (Widespread, British Isles & New World.):

> *In the name of heaven,*
> *The stars, and the moon,*
> *May I now dream,*
> *And that full soon*
> *If this I see.*
> *(Here, speak the wish.)*
> *Pray tell to me.*

* The plant known as Archangel grew where Mary touched the ground when she heard of Christ's coming, and so it is a blessed plant ever since, bringing hope and comfort. (Widespread, British Isles & New World.)

* A three-leaved clover brings good luck, but a four-leaved clover brings excellent luck and dispels all evil workings. (Widespread, British Isles & New World.)

* The rings that appear in old pastures where the grass seems brighter than the grass around it (caused by an invisible fungus beneath the surface) are called faery rings. It is here the faeries dance in circles under the moonlight. (Widespread, British Isles & New World.)

* Anyone whose eyes are anointed with the juice of the elder tree will be able to see spirits. (Widespread, British Isles.)

* The plant called agrimony, when laid under a pillow, causes a deep and pleasant sleep. (Widespread, British Isles.)

* With the first frost of the year, the Puca defecates on all of the blackthorn plants, so that anyone who picks its fruit after the first frost will fall ill. (Widespread, British Isles.)

* A cross made from rowan tree wood can ward off malefic witchcraft and evil spirits. (Scotland.)

* The smoke of smoldering juniper clears away evil spirits and bad luck. (Scotland.)

* A sprig of groundsel can keep away the evil eye. (Scotland.)

- A thistle plant growing near the home should be left to flower and thrive, for it will be a friend to you and warn of approaching enemies. (Scotland.)
- Foxglove flowers are worn by witches on the ends of their fingers. (Scotland.)
- Witches cure or bless patients by passing them nine times through garlands of woodbine. (Scotland.)
- A cross made of the wood of the mountain ash can ward off wicked spirits and witches. (New World.)
- Every year on October 10th, the Devil wanders about, spitting on every blackberry plant. Anyone who picks a blackberry after that date will suffer illness. (New World.)
- It is unlucky to cut down a whitethorn tree, for it is beloved of the faeries. (Ireland.)
- Faeries and witches ride the ragwort plant through the air in order to fly. (Ireland.)
- The flowers of the foxglove are used by the faeries to make their gloves. (Ireland.)
- Toadstools are called "faery tables," for the faeries sit and feast upon them. (Wales.)
- To cut down an entire oak tree brings grave illness and misfortune. (England.)
- No lightning bolt may strike a man who stands beside a bay tree. (England.)

- The fruits of the mallow plant are called "faery cheeses," for they are beloved by faeries. (England.)
- A clover of two leaves is useful for attracting love when placed in the right shoe. (England.)
- Ash leaves may be used in various ways for love charms, as in the following rhyme (England.)

> *The even ash leaf in my left hand,*
> *The first I meet be my husband;*
> *The even ash leaf inside my glove,*
> *The first I meet shall be my love;*
> *The even ash leaf upon my breast,*
> *The first I meet's whom I love best;*
> *The even ash leaf in my hand,*
> *The first I meet shall be my man.*
> *Even ash, I pluck from thee,*
> *This night my true love for to see.*
> *Neither in his rick nor rear,*
> *But in the clothes that he does wear.*

- Blackthorn and similar thorny, hedging plants, particularly when fortified with elder are known for their protective qualities, as in the saying, "an eldern stake and a blackthorn ether, will make a hedge to last forever." (England.)

- Wild parsley and hemlock are known for their malefic qualities, bringing ill luck and baneful curses, as in the saying, "where parsley's grown in the garden, there'll be a death before the year's out." Here, as in many other superstitions, "parsley" refers not to the common culinary herb, but to a dangerous look-alike. (England.)
- Rosemary empowers women who live nearby, as in the saying, "where rosemary flourishes, the lady rules." (England.)
- If a young woman wishes to dream of her future spouse, she should go to a young man's grave who died without being married and pick the yarrow plant, saying (England):

> *Yarrow, sweet yarrow, the first that I have found,*
> *In the name of Jesus Christ I pluck it from the ground;*
> *As Jesus loved sweet Mary and took her for His dear,*
> *So in a dream this night my true love will appear.*

- When a ring of fungus appears overnight in the countryside, this is sometimes called "hag tracks," referring to a spot where the spirits of witches dance about in the moonlight while their bodies are asleep in their beds. (England.)
- Ferns are used by faeries to secure oaths with magic. To kiss a fern and make a promise upon it ensures that the promise will be kept. (Cornwall.)

Superstitions of Beasts & Birds

- Killing spiders brings general misfortune, while letting them live brings good fortune, as in the saying, "If you wish to live and thrive, let a spider run alive." (Widespread, British Isles & New World.)
- A black cat crossing one's path indicates bad luck to follow. (Widespread, British Isles & New World.)
- Animals can see spirits. (Widespread, British Isles & New World.)

- A snake, no matter how it is killed, will not die until the sun goes down. (Widespread, British Isles & New World.)
- To carry a lucky hare's foot or rabbit's foot will protect against illness and dark workings. (Widespread, British Isles & New World.)
- A black cat passing by a window foretells the arrival of an unexpected guest. (Widespread, British Isles.)
- When the housecat washes on or around its ears, the weather will soon change. (Widespread, British Isles.)
- If a snake arrives at your front door, it predicts that someone in the household will die. (Widespread, British Isles.)
- To wear a snake skin hidden under your hat will ward off headaches. (Widespread, British Isles.)
- There is a secret bone in the head of a toad that, when found and kept, wards off evil. (Widespread, British Isles & New World.)
- There is a secret bone in a toad that allows one to control horses and other animals. (Widespread, British Isles.)
- If someone has a sore throat that will not pass, they may hold a frog to their throat, and then release it, and the frog will carry away the ailment. (Widespread, British Isles.)
- To slaughter a pig when the moon is waxing spoils the meat. (Widespread, British Isles.)
- It is unlucky to see a pig first thing in the morning. (Widespread, British Isles.)

- If you wish to have healthy farm animals, keep goats nearby, for they will soothe the other creatures and ward away illness. (England.)

- When you are on the road, count the white horses you see as you go along. If you reach 100, make a wish, and that wish will come true. (England.)

- Kill the first wasp that you see in the year, and your enemies' efforts will find no hold over you. (England.)

- During times of illness, leave all spiders to spin their webs about the home. It is said that a spider built a beautiful web once to protect Mary and her infant in the manger. (England.)

- To come across a piebald horse confers excellent luck. (Scotland.)

- If you see two piebald horses in a row, spit three times and make a wish. Your wish will come true. (Scotland.)

- To divine the one you will marry, set a snail upon a plate whereon you have scattered flour finely. Its trail will write the first letter of your beloved's name. (Ireland.)

- The Robin Redbreast plucked the sharpest thorn from Christ's head so that it no longer pained him, and his breast was stained with the blood. And so the Robin is lucky to this day and confers blessings. (Ireland.)

- Catch the first butterfly you see in the year, and you will overcome all of your enemies the rest of the year. (Cornwall.)

- A bird building a nest close to one's home brings good luck. (New World.)

- A bird that flies into a house brings bad luck. (New World.)
- To carry a hoe through a house brings the death of one's livestock. (New World.)
- A black cat crossing your path to the left brings bad luck. (New World.)
- A black cat crossing your path to the right brings good luck. (New World.)
- If a black cat takes up residence with a family, this indicates that any unmarried children are destined to marry well. (New World.)
- A cat resting on the front porch brings good luck to the home. (New World.)
- Kill a cat, and it will haunt you for the rest of your life. (New World.)
- A rabbit crossing one's path brings bad luck. (New World.)
- It brings good luck when two cats or two rabbits cross your path at night. (New World.)
- If a cow lows in front of one's door, there will be a death in the family. (New World.)
- Milk a cow onto the ground, and its milk will run dry. (New World.)
- If a dog stares at you and howls at midnight, you will be murdered. (New World.)
- If a dog howls twice at midnight, a woman will die. (New World.)
- If a dog howls three times at midnight, a man will die. (New World.)

- A dog growling in your path indicates bad luck for the journey ahead. (New World.)
- Drink the milk of a sow, and you will be able to see the wind. (New World.)
- See a white horse, and you will receive money before the end of the week. (New World.)
- Kill a toad, and your cow will give no more milk. (New World.)
- Bury a toad alive, and you will see spirits. (New World.)
- To pass a flock of geese brings good luck. (New World.)
- If a honeybee flies before your path, you will receive a letter. (New World.)
- A cricket brings luck when it enters a house. (New World.)
- To kill a daddy long-legs brings the death of one's livestock. (New World.)
- To find a spider crawling on you brings good luck. (New World.)
- To find a spider on your clothes brings good fortune; it indicates that the spider is spinning your wealth. (New World.)
- A black snake living nearby will drive away bad luck from a property. (New World.)

Superstitions of Spirits & the Dead

- To see a double of oneself is an omen of death. (Widespread, British Isles & New World.)
- To see a spectral black dog is an omen of death. (Widespread, British Isles & New World.)
- To see a vision of a woman in all white is an omen of death. (Widespread, British Isles & New World.)

- To step on a grave may anger the dead and bring their wrath down upon you. (Widespread, British Isles & New World.)
- Lights moving about land and sea denote the presence of a wicked spirit. (Widespread, British Isles & New World.)
- To obtain a lock of hair from the corpse of someone who loved you in life can confer blessings in the years to come, but to lose it brings dire misfortune. (Widespread, British Isles & New World.)
- When someone dies in the home, all mirrors must be covered with cloth or turned to face the wall so that the soul of the departed does not become lost in them. (Widespread, British Isles & New World.)
- Death may be convinced to delay his work and leave a person living until the ebb of the tide. (Widespread, British Isles & New World.)
- More people die during the new moon than any other time. (Widespread, British Isles & New World.)
- After a death, all clocks in the home must be stopped so that the dead do not linger after their time is up. (Widespread, British Isles & New World.)
- The bones of murdered men confer power and strength to those who touch them. (Widespread, British Isles.)
- Every family has its own "death warner," a spirit that appears to a particular family to warn them of impending death or danger. (Widespread, British Isles.)

- Will-o-wisps, also known as fetch-lights or corpse candles, are omens of death. (Widespread, British Isles.)
- Wherever a murdered man's boots are buried, there shall his ghost wander in the afterlife. (Ireland.)
- To have a house ghost and treat it politely brings good luck. (Ireland.)
- The spirits of the dead can take the form of hares, birds, or other animals, and so continue visiting their favorite places. (Ireland.)
- It is bad luck to speak ill around a corpse, for the dead can still hear everything that happens around the body. (Ireland.)
- The spirits of the dead can be chased away for some time by standing barefoot and snapping one's fingers at midnight. (Scotland.)
- Wicked spirits can be diverted by placing three beans in one's mouth, then walking at night in the open air, casting them behind one by one without looking back, then saying, "with these beans, I ransom myself." (Scotland.)
- If the specter of an absent person is seen in the morning, they will live long; if seen in the evening, they will die soon. (Scotland.)
- To place a gold watch in the palm of a dying person will buy them more time, for death will pause his work at this gesture—but not for long. (Scotland.)
- A haunted house can be cleared of its spirits by striking metal against metal nine times loudly. (Scotland.)

♦ If one passes over a bridge after midnight, they are sure to see three ladies sitting upon it wearing green dresses. (Wales.)

♦ A criminal hanged for his crimes will always come back as a vengeful spirit. (Wales.)

♦ To release the spirit of someone recently deceased from the home, open all of the windows and doors, unlock every lock, open all boxes, drawers, and trunks, and untie every knot. (England.)

♦ When a member of the family dies, a portion of every food served at the funeral feast must be taken out and offered to the bees living on the property. (England.)

♦ If someone dies holding a grudge against an enemy who wronged them, the vengeance of the dead can be exacted upon the living by tapping an object on their coffin three times, then casting it onto the property of the offender. (England.)

♦ Many phenomena may be signs or omens of an impending death in a home or community (England):

-Dogs howling at midnight.

-Cocks crowing before midnight.

-Hens crowing.

-A cow or mare birthing twins.

-The death-watch beetle ticking.

-Fruit trees blossoming out of season.

-Dreaming of being at a friend's wedding.

-An owl beating against the window.

-The sound of a bell in the ear.

* If a picture falls from the wall, the house has spirits. (New World.)
* Paint the porch ceiling "haint blue," and no wicked spirits can enter the home. (New World.)
* One should cross one's fingers when passing by a cemetery to ward off death. (New World.)
* A seventh son is able to see ghosts and spirits of all kinds. (New World.)
* If anyone dies in a family, one must tell the bees living on the property, or else they may be offended. (New World.)
* Death comes in threes. That is, death never takes only one or two. (New World.)
* One child in each family is able to conjure knocking spirits. (New World.)
* It is bad luck to speak ill of the dead, for anywhere the dead are spoken of by those who remember them, they are conjured, and can take vengeance. (New World.)
* If a wicked spirit is pursuing you, stop in the middle of a stream and make the sign of the cross, and it will depart. (New World.)
* If you are about at night and see the light known as the will o' wisp, turn your coat inside out to prevent evil spirits from harming you. (New World.)
* A white moth flying around you means the spirit of a grandparent is near. (New World.)

- If you are out alone at night, and you hear your name called, do not answer, for the spirits are calling you to join them. (New World.)
- Take a lock of hair from a corpse, and stuff it into a hole drilled into a tree, and the spirit will live on the land forever. If you remove the hair, the spirit will haunt you. (New World.)

Superstitions of the Black Art & Its Defense

- If you speak the Lord's Prayer backwards, you will conjure the Devil. (Widespread, British Isles & New World.)
- Carrying steel or iron protects against wicked spirits. (Widespread, British Isles & New World.)
- To cross one's fingers wards away evil influences. (Widespread, British Isles & New World.)

- To throw salt into a fire disrupts evil magic and wicked spirits. (Widespread, British Isles.)
- Throw salt over your left shoulder in order to remove bad luck. (Widespread, British Isles & New World.)
- To set a horseshoe over the door with its two ends pointing up will ward off evil and collect good luck. (Widespread, British Isles & New World.)
- A knot tied in one's hair can deter malevolent witchcraft. (Widespread, British Isles & New World.)
- A boom set beside the door will deter evil influences from entering. (Widespread, British Isles & New World.)
- To knock on wood repels all manner of bad luck, evil sorcery, and hateful spirits. (Widespread, British Isles & New World.)
- A wreath of rowan can protect against harmful witchcraft. (Wales.)
- A slit made in the ear of a newborn calf will protect it against evil witches. (Wales.)
- Spitting upon the floor at the mention of dark spirits will divert their influence. (Wales.)
- A door that has been painted white cannot be entered by the Devil or any dark spirit. (Wales.)
- A bag of salt in the cradle will protect babies from harm. (Wales.)
- If you walk three times backwards around a room at midnight, then gaze into a glass, you will see the Devil's face staring back at you. (England.)

♦ A particular property or plot of land may be cursed forever by laying a pile of stones in a hearth or firepit and declaring aloud that until the entire heap is burned, the land and all who own it and dwell upon it be cursed. The stones are then cast about the property in various places so that they may never be recovered. (England.)

♦ The nightmare may be warded off with the following curious "spell-song:" (England.)

> *Arthur Knight, he rode at night*
> *With open sword and candlelight.*
> *He sought the mare; he found the mare.*
> *He bound the mare with her own hair;*
> *And thus he made the mare to swear:*
> *That she would never bide at night*
> *Wherever she heard of Arthur Knight.*

♦ To point or gesture with the forefinger can be used in cursing, while the thumb can be used to bless or protect. (Scotland.)

♦ To "cross" oneself with the thumb protects against evil influences. (Scotland.)

♦ A cross made of rowan wood will protect against wicked spirits and dark witchcraft. (Scotland.)

- The blood of black-coated creatures (sheep, dogs, etc.), when smeared on one's doorframe, will ward away the powers of evil. (Scotland.)

- To become a witch, one must place one hand over one's head and the other hand under one's foot, and pledge everything between one's hands to the Devil. (Scotland.)

- To thwart evil spells and the workings of malevolent witches, reach for a piece of iron and touch it, saying the words "cold iron." (Scotland.)

- Witches may kill by throwing "elf bolts," which are arrowheads carved of stone, at their victims while traveling about invisibly in spirit form. (Scotland.)

- A bit of iron carried on one's person will prevent the workings of malevolent witches and evil spirits. (Scotland.)

- To become a witch, you must stand on the foot of another witch, who will place their hand on your head, and you must look over their left shoulder. (Ireland.)

- When one has died, and the suspected cause is black magic, one may sprinkle one's doorway with the blood of a hen in order to send the curse away. (Ireland.)

- Spit over your left shoulder to undo an evil charm. (New World.)

- Make a cross and spit in it for protection and good luck. (New World.)

- To write one's name in red ink brings either death, or the Devil, or both. (New World.)

- Place a dime in the heel of your shoe, and no one can place a curse on you. (New World.)
- To become a witch, one must shoot the moon nine times with a silver bullet, cursing God each time. (New World.)
- To become a witch, you must take a spinning wheel to a hill and promise yourself to the Devil. When the wheel begins to turn, the Devil has agreed. (New World.)
- To become a witch, one goes to the highest hill at sunrise nine days in a row and curses God. The Devil then places one hand on the person's head and the other under their feet, and the witch has to promise to the Devil everything between his two hands. (New World.)
- Witches often take the form of black cats to travel about in spirit form. (New World.)
- Witches may kill by rolling animal hair between their fingers into a small, hard, round ball, which they throw at their victims. (New World.)
- Witches may steal the milk of another person's cow by milking a cloth or tassel into a bowl. (New World.)
- If you are out and about in the world and sense evil spirits working against you, turn your hat backwards on your head, and they will be confused. (New World.)
- If a witch or evil charmer is tormenting you with their magic, draw a picture of them, and shoot it through with a silver bullet. (New World.)

- If someone is bewitched, gather nine willow twigs and bundle them together. Each day, remove one willow twig from the bundle, and before the ninth day, they will be cured. (New World.)

- A circle drawn about oneself with a forked willow branch will keep away malevolent spirits and hateful witches. (New World.)

- To break a witch's charm, spit on bristled end of a broom, and brush it over ashes in the fireplace. Then set it over the front door. The witch can do you no harm no longer, unless you give them something from your household. (New World.)

Superstitions of Days & Festivals

- To give alms or charity on Christmas brings excellent luck throughout the year to come. (Widespread, British Isles & New World.)
- Any water collected from a stream or well on Easter morning will be imbued with magical properties, and may be kept throughout the rest of the year for healing and blessing. (Widespread, British Isles & New World.)

* It brings good luck for anyone to bring newborn life into the house on Easter, be it an infant, a lamb, a calf, a piglet, a duckling, a young hare, etc. (Widespread, British Isles & New World.)

* To eat blackberries after All Hallows' Eve brings evil. (Widespread, British Isles.)

* If a bird sings on St. Brigid's Day (February 1st), this is a sign of good weather and good luck in the year ahead. (Widespread, British Isles.)

* Dreams on Midsummer Eve are powerful and predict the future. (Widespread, British Isles.)

* To collect herbs on Midsummer grants them great potency in healing, but no plants must be collected after sunset, for they will bring harm. (Widespread, British Isles.)

* People who are born on St. John's Eve (June 23rd) can see and converse with spirits. (Widespread, British Isles.)

* If one jumps over a fire on St. John's Eve (June 23rd), he will conquer his enemies. (Widespread, British Isles.)

* On noon, on Midsummer Day, one can find a rare stone under a plantain plant which will not appear at any other time. This should be kept and placed beneath one's pillow to dream of the future. (Widespread, British Isles.)

* The unburned portion of any candle lit on Candlemas can be used the remainder of the year to chase away evil influences and malicious spirits. (Widespread, British Isles.)

- "Yule straw" is imbued with magical protective powers, and any animals that lie on straw laid down on Christmas Day will be protected for the year to come. Likewise, any yule straw laid over the earth will make the soil beneath it fertile and rich for year's crops. (Widespread, British Isles.)
- An oak log, or Yule log, burned throughout the Christmas season will render ashes with magical properties. These ashes should be saved in order to mark things with good luck. (Widespread, British Isles.)
- If a cake baked for anyone on Christmas breaks in the middle, they will die before the next Christmas comes. (Scotland.)
- It is unlucky to spend any money on the first Monday after the New Year. (Scotland.)
- At midnight on New Year's Eve, go to the town well, and draw from it the first bucket of clean water for the new year, then let your cows drink from it. Your cows will give more and better milk than all your neighbors. (Scotland.)
- On All Hallows' Eve, take a shirt and dip one of its sleeves in a south-running stream that touches lands owned by three different people. Hang the shirt to dry by a fire, and sleep beside it, and you will see visions of your future mate. (Scotland.)
- On New Year's Day, to allow a guest to enter your home with nothing to offer brings bad luck for the year ahead. (Scotland.)
- To eat eggs on Easter brings excellent luck. (Scotland.)

♦ To bathe in a natural body of water at midnight on Lammas Day (August 1st) washes away bad luck and sickness, but the spirit of the water should be repaid with a coin before leaving. (Scotland.)

♦ To kiss chains on Lammas Day (August 1st) cures diseases of the throat. (Scotland.)

♦ To bake bread on Lammas Day (August 1st) brings good fortune to all in the home. (Scotland.)

♦ The first person to enter a home in the New Year (and the qualities this person possesses, be they kind or cruel, witty or stupid, etc.) will determine the luck of the family for the rest of the year. (Scotland.)

♦ It is lucky to eat eggs or milk on May Day. (Scotland.)

♦ On All Hallows' Eve, set pairs of nuts near in heat of the hearth, one pair for every couple whose future is to be divined. If the pair roast side by side, this bodes well. If one flies away from the other, their future together is not so certain. (Scotland.)

♦ Anything that can be cleaned before the New Year should be made spotless in order to bring good luck for the year ahead. (Scotland.)

♦ The weather on Candlemas day can be read to divine the weather for the coming weeks (Scotland):

> *If Candlemas Day be fair and clear,*
> *There'll be two winters in the year;*
> *If Candlemas Day bring clouds and rain,*
> *Winter will not come again.*

- Animals blessed on St. Stephen's Day (December 26th, or the Second Day of Christmas) will be healthy and protected throughout the coming year. (Wales.)
- It is lucky to wear a leek in or on the hat on March 1st. (Wales.)
- To bring home bread on Good Friday ensures success throughout the year. (Wales.)
- On May Day, fasten a green bough of a tree to your home, and you will have plenty of milk throughout the year. (Ireland.)
- If one's milk or butter is stolen on May Day, they will receive your prosperity throughout the rest of the year. (Ireland.)
- If one dreams of visiting a place on St. John's Eve (June 23rd), that is the place one will die one day. (Ireland.)
- On the Twelfth Night of Christmas, set a large bowl full of oats with twelve candles in a circle and one larger candle in the middle, then light them all in order to have good luck throughout the year. (Ireland.)
- Pluck a rose on St. John's Day (June 24th) at midnight, and wear it about throughout the day to bring love into your life. (Cornwall.)
- On St. Agnes' Eve (January 20th), take rosemary and thyme, and speak the following rhyme to ensure a happy marriage: "St. Agnes, that's to lovers kind, Come ease the troubles of my mind." (England.)
- New Year's Day is especially propitious for bible-dipping, in which the pages of the bible are flipped through quickly and blindly, and

a finger is dropped on a page in order to divine a message about the future from the words found there. (England.)

+ To enter any investment, transaction, or to offer loans on St. David's Day (March 1st) is very lucky, and ensures a good financial outcome. (England.)

+ A child born on Christmas Day will be able to speak with animals. (New World.)

+ Look into a mirror at midnight on Halloween, and you will see your future love. (New World.)

+ On Halloween, name an apple hung up by a string after a person you wish to have for your sweetheart. If you can bite it, they will be yours. (New World.)

+ If one can steal something on Christmas Day and get away with it, one will be a successful thief on any other day of the year to come. (New World.)

+ Go out to an old well on May Day, and look into an inverted mirror over its water in order to see your future. If you see a person, that is your future mate. If you see a casket, you will never marry. (New World.)

+ Walk out into a cornfield on Christmas Eve, and you will be informed of all happenings in your town throughout the year ahead. (New World.)

+ To eat pancakes on Ash Wednesday brings excellent luck. (New World.)

♦ On Halloween, one may set thirteen apples, called a Devil's dozen, in a tub of water, and participants then take turns "bobbing for apples." To pluck an apple from the water with only your teeth wins the game, at which point one may make a wish that will surely come true. (New World.)

♦ Go out on May Day before breakfast without speaking a single word, and take a bridle from the barn, saying three times, "Here is a bridle; where is the horse and rider?" You will see a vision of your future spouse. (New World.)

♦ The Dog Days (late summer, generally mid-July through mid-August) bring madness in dogs, and it is dangerous to wander about alone during this time. (New World.)

♦ The Easter egg hunt, in which many parties, usually children, hunt for eggs painted various colors, was at one time used to foretell the future, as in the following rhyme (New World):

> *The one who gets a golden egg*
> *Will plenty have and never beg.*
>
> *The one who gets an egg of blue*
> *Will find a sweetheart fond and true.*
>
> *The one who gets an egg of green*
> *Will jealous be and not serene.*

The one who gets an egg of black,
Bad luck and troubles ne'er will lack.

The one who gets an egg of white
In life shall find supreme delight.

The one who gets an egg of red
Will many tears of sorrow shed.

Who gets an egg of purple shade
Will die a bachelor or old maid.

A silver egg will bring much joy
And happiness without alloy.

The lucky one is the egg of pink.
The owner ne'er sees danger's brink.

The one who gets an egg of brown
Will have establishment in town.

The one who speckled egg obtains
Will go through life by country lanes.

A striped egg bodes care and strife,

A sullen man or scolding wife.

The one who gets an egg of plaid,
His heart is good, but luck is bad.

107

.

Bibliography

Addy, S. O. (1880). *Household Tales with Other Traditional Remains.*

Aubrey, J. (1696). *Miscellanies upon Various Subjects.*

Caldwell, O. W. & Gerhard, E. L. (1934). *Do You Believe It?*

Chambers, R. (1864). *The Book of Days.*

D'Abano, P. (1500s). *Heptameron, or Magical Elements.*

Daniels, C. L. & Stevens, C. M. (1903). *Encyclopedia of Superstitions, Folk-Lore, and Occult Sciences of the World.* Volume 1.

Daniels, C. L. & Stevens, C. M. (1903). *Encyclopedia of Superstitions, Folk-Lore, and Occult Sciences of the World.* Volume 2.

Daniels, C. L. & Stevens, C. M. (1903). *Encyclopedia of Superstitions, Folk-Lore, and Occult Sciences of the World.* Volume 3.

Deerforth, D. (1928). *Knockwood: Superstition Through the Ages.*

Eichler, L. (1924). *The Customs of Mankind.*

Fielding, W. J. (1943). *Strange Superstitions and Magical Practices.*

Fiske, J. (1887). *Myths and Myth-Makers.*

Folklore Society. (1878-). *Folk-Lore Record.* (Multiple journal volumes.)

Folklore Society. (1878-). *Folklore.* (Multiple journal volumes.)

Folklore Society. (1878-). *Folk-Lore Journal.* (Multiple journal volumes.)

Gomme, G. L. (1884). *The Gentleman's Magazine Library: Popular Superstitions.*

Gunnyon, W. (1879). *Illustrations of Scottish History, Life, and Superstition from Song and Ballad.*

Igglesden, C. (1931). *Those Superstitions.*

Knowlson, T. S. (1910). *The Origins of Popular Superstitions and Customs.*

Kunz, G. F. (1913). *The Curious Lore of Precious Stones.*

Mackay, C. (1852). *Extraordinary Popular Delusions and the Madness of Crowds.*

Olcott, W. T. (1911). *Star Lore of All Ages.*

Olcott, W. T. (1914). *Sun Lore of All Ages.*

Stimpson, G. (1946). *A Book About a Thousand Things.*

Sumner, W. G. (1929). *Folkways.*

Swainson, C. (1866). *The Folklore and Traditional Names of British Birds.*

Thiselton-Dyer, T. F. (1889). *The Folk-Lore of Plants.*

Thomas, D. L. (1920). *Kentucky Superstitions.*